T0078095

PAKISTAN PROBLEMS, SOLUTIONS

*To recognize Pakistan's main problems
and propose possible solutions*

AGHA S. HAMID ZAMAN

Archway Publishing books may be ordered through booksellers or by contacting:

Archway Publishing
1663 Liberty Drive
Bloomington, IN 47403
www.archwaypublishing.com
844-669-3957

ISBN: 978-1-6657-2032-8 (sc)
ISBN: 978-1-6657-2033-5 (e)

Library of Congress Control Number: 2022904577

Print information available on the last page.

Archway Publishing rev. date: 04/13/2022

"In the name of God, the Most Gracious, the Most Merciful."

CONTENTS

FOREWORD

The book tries to list out main problems facing Pakistan. It also tries to propose optimum solutions to those problems.

Neither the list of problems is exhaustive nor are the proposed solutions unique. What is put out is an opinion.

Opinions can always differ. The purpose is to give food for thought and initiate debate and dialogue.

WHY THIS BOOK?

Agha Sher Hamid Zaman

I was born in January 1947. The same year Pakistan came into being. My parents and my grandfather migrated to Pakistan from Hoshiarpur East Punjab. My grandfather Sher Zaman Khan owned a car in mid 1940s. Beside that our family had tremendous inherited urban and rural property in Hoshiarpur.

Despite being very rich, they were well educated and served in government. My grandfather retired around 1920 as Inspector of Police. My maternal grandfather also retired as Inspector of Police in early 1900s. At that time generally only the British occupied that position in Police.

My father did his Masters in Psychology from Punjab University through Forman Christen College Lahore in 1934. Later in 1953 he did his Phd in Psychotherapy (by mailing a written thesis) from England in 1953. He served in Education Department and retired as Divisional Inspector of Schools.

After migration to Lahore in September 1947 my grandfather rented two rooms on first floor in "Purani Anarkali" Lahore. The family bought aluminum utensils for cooking and eating. They did not grab any house or property on their own and depended on whatever was allotted to them by the government. It was almost nothing as compared to what they had left behind. They would also not bribe anybody, whatever the cost.

I have been a witness to the trauma of what they thought they were migrating to and what Pakistan, unfortunately developed into. They felt always optimistic about Pakistan, however they died completely disillusioned. I have seen Pakistan gradually deteriorate in all aspects, economic, moral, education and what not.

I have worked in high management positions in both government and private sectors and abroad as well. I have travelled extensively in North America, Europe, Middle East, Far-East including Singapore, Malaysia, China, Japan, and Australia. Since some time, I have been studying and trying to bring to fore some problems that Pakistan is facing today and also trying to put out my suggestions on what to do about them. The effort is not supposed to be exhaustive but pretty much covers the main problems and proposed solutions. The solutions suggested cannot be unique. It is an opinion. Opinions can differ. This is meant to serve as food for thought and initiate debate, dialogue and useful suggestions.

WHAT THE BOOK CONTAINS?

The book is not supposed to be exhaustive in listing the problems. The suggested solutions are also not supposed to be unique. It tries to discuss the main problems Pakistan faces today and possible solutions in the form of an opinion. Opinions can always differ. It is important to debate a point freely, consider consequences and hammer out what is the best way.

The chapters of the book are listed below:

- Population Growth
- Fiscal Deficits
- External Debt, Foreign Exchange Reserves, Rupee Value
- Corruption
- Unemployment
- Intolerance, Extremism, Moral Degradation
- Education
- Lack of Democratic Process in History
- Lack of Clean water and Non Focus on Agriculture

Initially the material was put out as Blogsite in mid-August 2018. It was updated yearly. The last updated version was put out in January 2021. The link to the blogsite is:

https://pakistanproblemssolutions.home.blog/

Contact Information:

Agha S. Hamid Zaman
Email: hamid-zaman@hotmail.com

Agha S. Hamid Zaman has following profiles:

Agha S. Hamid Zaman | LinkedIn
Agha S. Hamid Zaman | Facebook

POPULATION GROWTH

As on 13 January 2021 Pakistan's population was over 223 million. Current growth rate is 2%. We are 5th largest country of the world by population. Having a land area of 770,880 square Kilometers or 297, 638 Sq. Miles, population density is 287 per Sq. Km Urban population is 35%. Median age is 22.8 years. In 1970, total population of both the wings amounted to 132 million. At that time East Pakistan had a population of 72 million and West Pakistan had a population of 60 million. Pakistan has grown in population from 60 million to over 222 million from 1970 to 2020. Pakistan's current yearly population growth rate is 2%. Bangladesh's rate is 1%, India is at 1%, USA is at 0.7%. Population growth rate in China is 0.5% while in Japan it is negative at-0.1%.

POSSIBLE WAYS TO CONTROL EXPONENTIAL GROWTH OF POPULATION

1. Awareness:

People have to be told about consequences of having too many children. They must be made to understand that if they have less number of children they would be able to feed them and educate and take care of them more easily in a quality way.

2. Education & development

Education especially of women makes them understand the consequences of having large number of children. Development like availability of basic health facilities and reduction of poverty especially in rural areas can help reduce population growth.

3. Incentives

Providing incentives for having one child or two child families can be and has been a successful way of controlling population. Taxing people with more children or providing financial incentives like allowances and free education to small family cases could be effective. This would require proper legislation and strict implementation.

4. Avoidance of early age marriages

Early age marriages provide a larger span of having births. Also it denies the proper education. Legislation to fix a minimum age of marriage could probably help.

References

https://en.wikipedia.org/wiki/Demographic_history_of_Pakistan

http://www.worldometers.info/world-population/pakistan-population

https://www.nytimes.com/1970/04/12/archives

FISCAL DEFICITS

Budget Deficit

No entity, whether a government or a household, can run with a mounting deficit for very long without chaos. Pakistan's budget after the 1990s started to run into a deficit. The situation compounded after 2004. During the fiscal year of July 2019 to June 2020, our budget deficit was Rs. 3,376 billion.

Fiscal Year	Total Revenue (Trillion Rupees)	Total Expenditure (Trillion Rupees)	Deficit (Trillion Rupees)	Percent of GDP
2019-2020	6.272	9.648	3.376	5.8%
2018-2019	4.900	8.345	3.445	8.9
2017-2018	5.230	7.448	2.260	6.6

Budget Deficit during the last fifty years (at end of June 2020, the deficit was 3,376 billion rupees).

Important expenditure heads during 2019–2020 were debt servicing (2.619 trillion), defense (1.213 trillion), PSDP (1.090 trillion), education (83.164 billion), and health (11.439 billion). GDP growth in year 2018 was 5.53 percent. In the year 2019, the growth rate dropped to 1.91 percent.

Total debt and liabilities of public sector enterprises (PSEs) was Rs. 1.711 billion. During fiscal year 2017–2018 it was 1.394 billion.

Major contributors to the PSE debt are PIA (141.8 billion), WAPDA (67.4 billion), and Pakistan Steel Mills (43.2 billion). Other miscellaneous PSEs contribute 1,232.5 billion rupees. Liabilities of PSEs at the end of June 2020 were 221.27 billion rupees.

In the first quarter of 2020, PIA earnings were Rs. 36,445 million. During this period, loss before taxation was Rs. 17,389 million. During the calendar year of 2019, PIA revenue was 147,500 million rupees, while losses before tax was 54,954 million rupees. During the calendar year of 2018, PIA revenue was 103,490 million rupees, and losses before tax was 67,418 million rupees.

Pakistan Railways was another contributor to PSE's ordeal. In the fiscal year of 2018–2019, its revenue was 54.59 billion and net loss was 32.59 billion rupees. Railways have 7,791 kilometers of track, 72,078 employees, and it catered to 70 million passengers.

Circular debt

Circular debt is the accumulation of defaulted payments by power distribution companies to power producers who then default on making payments to their gas and oil suppliers.

That means power producers are unable to produce electricity, which means distributors do not deliver enough electricity, which means the consumer refuses to pay their bill because they are not receiving power. On top of this, the government owes unpaid subsidies to power-distributing companies, and one also has to contend with theft and operational inefficiencies within the system.

In June 2018 the country's total circular debt was Rs. 1,126 billion, which has gone up to Rs. 2,150 billion as of June 30, 2020.

CURRENT ACCOUNT DEFICIT

A current account deficit shows that a country's balance of payments has imported more goods and services than it exported, including other foreign exchange receipts like remittances.

There are four components of the current account. The largest is trade in goods and services. The other three are much smaller. Net income is earned by residents by overseas investments or work. Second are direct remittances from workers to their home country, foreign aid, and foreign direct investments. The third is increases or decreases in assets like banks deposits, securities, and real estate.

Pakistan recorded a current account surplus of USD 778 million in the third quarter of 2020.

Current account balance posted a surplus of 778 million dollars in the third quarter of 2020. However in January 2022, the Current Account Deficit hit an all-time high of USD 2.55 Billion. During the fiscal year of 2019–2020, Pakistan exported USD 22,507 million. Imports during the same period were USD 42,417 million. The trade deficit during July 2019 to June 2020 was USD 19,910 million. Pakistan recorded a trade deficit of PKR 284,315 million in August of 2020. Imports were 549,852 million rupees.

Exports were 265,537 million. Remittances were 6,122 million. Foreign direct investment was 120 million rupees.

Pakistan imported USD 37.3 billion worth of goods in 2019. The following is a list of the main imports during 2019:

Machinery, including computers: $5 billion (13.3 percent of total imports)

Electrical machinery equipment: $4.6 billion (12 percent)

Iron, steel: $2.3 billion (6.1 percent)

Mineral fuels, including oil: $2.2 billion (5.9 percent)

Organic chemicals: $2 billion (5.2 percent)

Plastics, plastic articles: $1.8 billion (4.7 percent)

Cotton: $1.7 billion (4.4 percent)

Manmade filaments: $1.5 billion (3.9 percent)

Vehicles: $1.2 billion (3.1 percent)

Oil seeds: $1 billion (2.7 percent)

Pakistan exported an estimated $20.8 billion worth of goods around the globe in 2019.

The following is a list of major exports from Pakistan in 2019:

Miscellaneous textiles, worn clothing: $4.2 billion (20 percent of total exports)

Clothing, accessories (not knit or crochet): $3.5 billion (16.7 percent)

Knit or crochet clothing, accessories: $3.3 billion (16.1 percent)

Cotton: $1.8 billion (8.4 percent)

Cereals: $1.2 billion (5.9 percent)

Leather/animal gut articles: $716.7 million (3.5 percent)

Copper: $596.7 million (2.9 percent)

Optical, technical, medical apparatus: $421 million (2 percent)

Mineral fuels including oil: $393.8 million (1.9 percent)

Fish: $372.5 million (1.8 percent)

References

http://finance.gov.pk/fiscal/July June 2019 20.pdf

https://tradingeconomics.com/pakistan/government-budget-value

https://www.thenews.com.pk/print/708319-debt-of-pses-increases-6-9pc-to-rs1-490-trillion-in-fy2020

https://www.dawn.com/news/1578030

https://www.brecorder.com/news/40016435

https://www.piac.com.pk/corporate/images/corporate reports/1ˢᵗ-Quarter-Report-2020.pdf

http://www3.piac.com.pk/Downloads/PIA ANNUAL REPORT 2019.PDF

https://en.wikipedia.org/wiki/Pakistan Railways

https://www.sbp.org.pk/ecodata/PSEs.pdf

https://profit.pakistantoday.com.pk/2020/07/18/circular-debt-the-nearly-2-trillion-problem/

https://www.sbp.org.pk/ecodata/exp import BOP.pdf

HOW TO ELIMINATE
FISCAL DEFICITS

1. Stop the drain.

The financial managers of the country have to make hard decisions in getting rid of the loss-making public sector entities. It would be hard to reform the existing entities. Specific legislation to curb it being challenged in courts plus strict law enforcement could help. This would require understanding among all institutions of the state. Also, all national organizations have to be headquartered in Islamabad.

2. Abolish all subsidies.

All subsidies except the ones in agriculture have to be abolished. Services like the metro have to be made profitable. Consider enhancing the ticket from Rs. 20 to Rs. 100–200 to get rid of the deficit; it has to be increased accordingly.

3. Document the economy; eliminate cash economy.

The economy must be fully computerized in all aspects. All bank accounts could be tracked for inflow and outflow. All transactions above a certain amount should be tracked. All property purchases and existing records of properties have to be put on the computer for tracking. Similarly, all purchases of expensive cars have to be recorded. We must put in place all these measures to control and finish off the cash economy. Discontinuation of high-denomination notes may also be considered.

4. Reform tax system by reducing taxes and duties.

Taxation in Pakistan is very complex. There are more than seventy different taxes and nearly thirty-seven different government agencies administer the tax system. Only 1.9 million people pay taxes. Tax to GDP ratio was 9.5 percent in 2019–2020—falling compared with the previous two years.

Simplify the tax system by reducing the number of taxes. Reduce tax rates and duties drastically. Abolish all discretionary powers. High duties and taxes induce people to avoid tax and encourage corruption. Suggestions on some major taxes and duties are below.

We have had high rates of income tax, corporate tax, sales tax, and regulatory duties. It has not helped the country. People tend to avoid the high rates. The cumbersome system, discretion, and interpretable rules compound the matter. It is high time we correct all those factors.

Income Tax

It is well known that most of the income tax is paid by salaried class. The current rate of income exempt from income tax is Rs. 400,000 per year. The maximum tax rate is 20 percent. The Islamic concept of income tax, zakat, is based on three basic principles: (1) It is voluntary and self-assessed, (2) the income that is genuinely used for sustaining your family's living is exempt, and (3) the income unused and accumulated over the year after supporting your family is subjected to a deduction of 2.5 percent for distribution among the needy. The system is very realistic and caters to human nature. It takes care of a person's family's living needs fairly, and the rate is low, at only 2.5 percent.

In current times, a couple living in their own house need normally 200,000 to make a reasonable living. A family with two children would need a minimum of Rs. 300,000 per month to sustain a reasonable living, even when the family owns the house in which they live. That means a family has to spend Rs. 3.6 million a year for living.

Our country's income tax allows only an exempt income at Rs. 400,000 for a full year, which is downright ridiculous. No wonder only the salaried class pays the tax. The maximum rate of income tax is now 20 percent, which is also very high and unrealistic.

If we follow the basic principles set by our religion, an income of Rs. 3–4 million per year should be exempt from income tax. The rate should also be reduced to a maximum of 2.5 percent. Every citizen then has to be asked to declare his or her income. Allowances can be made for if one does not own a house. We must also completely eradicate the cash economy and try to make it a completely documented economy.

Corporate Tax

The corporate tax in Pakistan has remained between 31–40 percent, which is also unrealistically high. No wonder the highest corporate tax payers in the country are public sector companies like OGDCL and PPL and GHPL. Corporate tax is zero in UAE. No wonder almost all business concerns now are basing their operations at least for the eastern hemisphere in UAE. To encourage business and industry and employment opportunities, we should reduce it to a maximum of 5 percent.

Sales Tax

Sales tax in Pakistan is 17 percent, which is why people try to avoid it with undocumented transactions. We should lower it to a maximum of 5 percent. This would encourage people to pay and transect legally.

Duties on Cars

The system of duties and taxes on cars in Pakistan is quite complicated. For new cars with engine capacities of 1,801–3,000 CC, the duty is 80 percent. In addition, a sales tax at 17 percent, an income tax at 5 percent, and an excise duty tax at 1 percent need to also be paid.

In India, the duty of newly imported, completely built-up unit (CBU) of over 3,000 CC is 100 percent, while those with less than 3,000 CC engine have a duty of 60 percent. In UAE the duty is 5 percent.

We should exempt hybrid and electric cars from duties and taxes. On normal nonhybrid cars, we should have a flat duty and tax rate combined at 50 percent for cars above 3,000 CC, and for cars below 3,000 CC it should be a flat 30 percent.

5. Controlling Trade Deficit:

We have to reduce our dependence on our main imports. Imported oil consumption can be reduced by encouraging use of hybrid and electric vehicles. Duties on electric cars should be abolished. Also decent public transport has to be made available from all residential areas to main work centers in major cities. This should reduce oil import as well as exponential use of personal vehicles. The local car manufactures must be made to offer quality cars at affordable price.

Things like computers and mobile phones should be manufactured in the country. But we must remember that cost and ease of doing business plus un interrupted availability of raw materials and energy has to ensured apart from consistent policies.

We must not import things like vegetables and fruits as we must encourage our agriculture and horticulture. These sectors should be made to learn to produce value added products for internal use as well as for export.

6. Circular Debt Elimination

Reduce transmission losses drastically.

Renegotiate capacity payments with power producers. Restructure billing slabs to protect domestic consumers, export oriented Industry and agriculture.

Reduce electricity rates. This would avoid theft and pilferage.

Reference

https://www.brecorder.com/news/40024644

7. Revenue Generation with Tourism

There would hardly be any country in the world which has ample history, excellent scenery, perpetual snow areas, glaciers, some highest mountains, vast planes, deserts, and sea beaches. Pakistan can have substantial increase in its revenues by promoting tourism by improving law and order situation and by improving infrastructure and improving available facilities.

Also we do have teach our people, especially men to lower their gaze as instructed to us by our religion.

EXTERNAL DEBT, FOREIGN EXCHANGE RESERVES, AND RUPEE VALUE

External Debt

As of March 2020, public debt of Pakistan is estimated to be about Rs42.8 trillion/US$256 billion which is 84 percent of gross domestic product (GDP) of Pakistan. About Rs18.17 trillion is owed by the government to domestic creditors, and about Rs13.78 trillion is owed by Public Sector Enterprises (PSEs).

As of March 2020, external Debt of Pakistan was around US$112 billion. Pakistan owes US$11.3 billion to Paris Club, US$27 billion to multilateral donors, US$5.765 billion to International Monetary Fund, and US$12 billion to international bonds such as Eurobond, and sukuk. About fifth of the external debt which is estimated around US$19 billion is owed to China due to China-Pakistan Economic Corridor.

Pakistan's debt history:

Pakistan received foreign assistance of US $ 121 million during 1951-1955. Later when the country became an ally in SEATO and CENTO the figure tripled in 5 years.

At the end of December 1969, the external debt of Pakistan had amounted to $2.7 billion including the debt of Bangladesh. Pakistan's total external debt was $3 billion by December 1971. Between December 1969 and December 2012, the external debt of Pakistan had jumped by 2,354 percent, from just $2.7 billion to $66.243 billion.

Pakistan's external debt was $21.9 billion in 1990, $22.8 billion in 1991, $24.8 billion in 1992, $27.6 billion in 1993, $31.1 billion in 1994, $32.7 billion in 1995, $34.7 billion in 1996, $35.8 billion in 1997, $35.8 billion in 1998, $36.5 billion in 1999 and $35.6 billion in 2000.

By the end of 2004, the total external debt was resting at $33 billion. At the end of June 2007, when General Musharraf was still in power, the loans had soared to $40.5 billion.

Between June 1999 and December 2012, Pakistan's foreign debt registered an upsurge of nearly 120 per cent, up from at $30.2 billion to a whopping $66.243 billion.

Ironically, during the first 60 years of its independence, the country's public debt had stood at just Rs4,802 billion!

Foreign Exchange Reserves

The foreign exchange reserves of the country were at $17.971 billion a week ago ended on June 26, 2020. The official reserves held by the SBP increased by $811 million to $12.042 billion by week ended July 03, 2020

Pakistan's Foreign Exchange Reserves at State Bank of Pakistan were at 13.9 USD billion in Aug 2020

Gold Reserves

Gold Reserves in Pakistan remained unchanged at 64.60 Tonnes in the second quarter of 2020 from 64.60 Tonnes in the first quarter of 2020.

RUPEE-US DOLLAR PARITY

Fiscal deficits, external debt and low level of foreign exchange Reserves affected the Rupee parity with the US dollar badly.

INFLATION

Inflation Rate in Pakistan during the last about 3 years has seen fluctuation from a low of 3.6% in March 2018 to a high of 14.6% in January 2020. In October 2020 it is hovering around 9%. People are generally unhappy about the rise in inflation rate.

Ongoing high inflation is a serious problem overlooked so far by the current government

References

https://www.sbp.org.pk/ecodata/profile.pdf
https://tradingeconomics.com/pakistan/external-debt
https://www.ceicdata.com/en/indicator/pakistan/external-debt
https://en.wikipedia.org/wiki/National_debt_of_Pakistan#
https://tradingeconomics.com/pakistan/gold-reserves
https://tradingeconomics.com/pakistan/inflation-

CORRUPTION

During year 2019, Pakistan ranked 120 out of 180 countries in corruption. Corruption perception Index was 32/100. We slightly deteriorated from a rank of 117 in year 2017. Pakistan reached an all-time high of 144 in 2005 and a record low of 39 in 1995.

There are ample laws that prohibit corruption. It is illegal to accept money by individuals or pay money to individuals under Pakistan Penal Code. The same applies to companies as per Prevetion of Corruption Act. Also acceptence of payment or receiving gifts is not allowed under National Accountability Ordinance.

Despite having a strong legal frame work the Government is unable to stop corruption especially in state entities because implementation of preventive laws is weak and ineffective. Corruption is a significant obstacle to business in Pakistan

The change in regimes between military and civilian also weakened the anti-corruption institutions. This may also be noted that a significant improvement in corruption in Pakistan has not occurred either in civilian government or in military government.

Two laws that are meant to prevent corruption in Pakistan are Prevention of Corruption Act and National Accountablitity

Ordinance (NAO). Both public sector and private sector come under preview of NAO. The NAO states that it is the owner of an assest who has to provide and prove legitimicy of its purchase and that any unexplained asset or assets wouldbe deemed as corruption. Abuse of office and money laundering is also under the law. AntiMoney Laudering Ordinance exists which prescribes upto ten years of prison term, fine and confisication of illlegally acquired asset in the name of the accused or or his or her dependents. Companies can also be held liable under all these laws.

Despite all this and more, corruption is wide spread in all spheres of life in Pakistan. Most effected sectors are public services, lower judiciary, land administration, tax administration, custom administration, public procurement, and what not.

In 2002, in a report titled "Nature and Extent of Corruption in the Public Sector", Transparency International (TI) Pakistan reported that the highest amounts of bribery were spent on people affiliated with the judiciary. Later in 2010, TI Pakistan presented a breakdown of the various actors in the judicial system involved in corruption. A majority of the participants reported that they, or someone in their household, has been subjected to an act of corruption while interacting with someone from the judiciary. When asked of the actors involved, 33.62% people said court employees, 23.73% said public prosecutors, 14.12% said witnesses,

12.43% said judges, 8.19% said opponent lawyer, 4.52% said magistrates while 3.39% mentioned others.

The lower level of the judiciary suffers from nepotism, influence from wealthy persons and influential religious and political figures, and corruption. In recent years the judiciary overreached, leading to increasing inefficiency and a very high workload leading to delays. Foreign investors usually prefer to include the options for international arbitration because of known delays and weakness of Pakistan's judiciary.

In a 2011 survey, TI Pakistan identified judiciary as the most corrupt institution in Pakistan alongside police. Nevertheless, with the proceedings of some high-impact corruption cases against government officials, including the prime minister, the Supreme Court demonstrated its positive role in tackling corruption.

Corruption is found to be commonplace in the lower levels of police. Police was observed as the most corrupt sector in a 2013 survey by Transparency International (TI). This situation has persisted since the graft watchdog's July 2010 survey, in which it was noted that the major cause for corruption in this sector was due to a lack of accountability and merit, and low salaries. Payment of bribes in order to escape and avoid charges was also commonplace; 31% of 4,224 respondents reported paying bribes to the police.

CURBING CORRUPTION

All religions prohibit corruption. The overwhelming majority of our population (96.3 percent) is Muslim. It is strange that despite vehemently calling ourselves Muslims, we hardly practice its teachings in daily life. Though corruption is so much prohibited in Islam, we seem to hardly care.

Training by Parents:

Strict indoctrination and training by parents from early age in differentiating between "halal" and "haram" and asking them to keep away from "haram" helps. Asking children to be afraid of Allah and making them believe that we are answerable to him one day also helps. It is clear that law of the land is no deterrent in so called developing countries where economic compulsions and the impression that one can get away with it are the luring factors.

Reforming Public Services Administration and Financial Management

Authority has to be matched with compensation. Officials in our public service entities enjoy immense power in exercising authority like transferring ownership of property to initiating or not initiating a case and so on. If the authority does not match the compensation the person exercising authority tends to get corrupt and arrogant. The government must realize that the person exercising authority has economic compulsions like having a home, reasonably good living, good education for children, and medical care of the family. Thus taking care of the person and his family's necessities must help.

Reducing Discretion, less human indulgence and transparency in documentation and de politicization of public services should help. We must hold Head of The Unit responsible to curb wrong doing. If the head of unit is honest, strong person who does not do any wrong then nobody under him can.

Closing international loopholes like transferring of money to overseas banks has to be curbed through help from other countries.

Internal decentralized accountability to fire corrupt persons immediately has to be legalized through legislation. Even Allah has a system of "saza" and "jaza".

References

https://tradingeconomics.com/pakistan/corruption-rank
https://www.business-anti-corruption.com/country-profiles/pakistan/
https://pakistancorruptionreport.wordpress.com/
https://en.wikipedia.org/wiki/Corruption_in_Pakistan
https://tradingeconomics.com/pakistan/corruption-index
https://www.transparency.org/news/feature/how_to_stop_corruption_5_key_ingredients

UNEMPLOYMENT

Unemployment refers to the share of the labor force that is without work but available for and seeking employment. Pakistan unemployment rate for 2019 was 4.45%, a 0.37% increase from 2018. Pakistan unemployment rate for 2018 was 4.08%, a 0.14% increase from 2017. Pakistan unemployment rate for 2017 was 3.95%, a 0.16% increase from 2016.

Less demand, more people available:

High population growth rate is mainly responsible for availability of more manpower than the demand in the shape of vacancies.

Deteriorating education and professional standards:

Lack of professional standards in education system causes persons with higher degrees unable to perform and practice professional skills.

Migration of people from rural to urban areas:

Large number of population migrates every year from rural to urban areas in search of jobs or whatever work they can get.

Lack of investment in Industries:

Normally industry setups provide maximum number of jobs in all countries. We must also incentivize set up of value added product industry in rural areas. During past several years there has been marked decrease in foreign and local investments in industries. The reasons for the decrease were terrorist threats, deterioration of law and order situation, lack of affordable and uninterrupted supply of electricity and gas, apart from the red tape and corrupt practices to get necessary approvals.

Controlling Unemployment:

Improve Standard of Education:

We must improve our standard of general education as well as professional education. It should be comparable to international standards. This would enhance the quality of available workforce.

Reconsideration of retirement age:

We should consider reduction of retirement age to make available vacancies at all levels.

De-politicization of government departments to prioritize merit rather than references:

We must de politicalize the government machinery and bureaucracy. We must also ensure that merit is essential to get a job rather than references.

Encourage value added industry setup in rural areas:

We must endeavor to setup value added products industry based on agriculture and horticulture in and very near to rural areas. This should ensure providing jobs to locals living in rural areas nearby.

Incentivize set up of manufacturing industries in affordable cost:

Any local or foreign investor would like to invest in a place where it can earn money. Speedy approvals without red tape or corrupt practices are a must. It would also require rule of law, peaceful situation, consistent and efficient regulatory and other government policies, relatively cheap skilled labor, supply of uninterrupted, affordable gas and electricity and water. The cost and ease of doing business and setting of industry in Pakistan has to be radically improved to reduce unemployment. Also we have to be at least regionally competitive rather a preferred destination in this regard.

Radically Improve Ease of Doing Business

No state can afford to provide jobs to all its citizens. It is usually the private sector industry and businesses that have to absorb and employ people. For this to happen, the private industry and businesses have to flourish. They flourish if they make money. Only then they can employ people.

For all this to happen we need to give tax holidays to new setups and cut taxes radically as suggested in last chapter. High taxes only encourage evasion and corruption. It has not worked and it would never ever work to increase government revenues.

Secondly we have to radically improve Ease of Doing Business. For this we have to simplify and ease the procedure to get regulatory approvals. The attitudes also have to change. Those at the helm must adopt a business friendly attitude. They have to discard the notion that they are doing any favour to the new setup. Rather any one or any group who is trying to invest in new industry or business is doing the country and its people a favour.

The Ease of doing business index ranks countries against each other based on how the regulatory environment is conducive to business operation stronger protections of property rights. Economies with a high rank (1 to 20) have simpler and friendlier regulations for businesses.

Ease of Doing Business in Pakistan

Pakistan is ranked 108 among 190 economies in the ease of doing business, according to the latest World Bank annual ratings. The rank of Pakistan improved to 108 in 2019 from 136 in 2018. In year 2008 and 2009 it was ranked at 85.

Gas and Electricity Tariffs for Business has to be reduced radically

No industry or business can make profit and flourish if the expanses for running it are high. We do have ample availability of work force.

The electricity and gas consumption rates for industry and business have to be made competitive, rather attractive regionally.

In Bangladesh, the industrial gas tariff is perhaps the lowest in the world at $3.61, which competes with the tariff in the US (shale gas) where it varies between $3.70 in winter and $5 in summer. Pakistan's industrial gas tariff is at $7 per MMBtu as compared with Bangladesh average tariff of $3.61 per MMBtu.

Here is a comparison of gas and electricity tariffs with other countries in the region.

Country	Electricity Rate per KWh	Gas Rate per MMBTU
Pakistan	0.157 USD	07.00 USD
Bangladesh	0.106 USD	03.61 USD
India	0.111 USD	03.23 to 08.43 USD

We have to reduce the tariffs to be an attractive destination for setting up new industry and business. Also we must improve and radically simplify the procedures to get new gas and electricity connections for new setups that have the possible capacity to employ people.

References

https://tribune.com.pk/story/2176787/review-gas-sector-prices
https://www.globalpetrolprices.com/
https://www.thenews.com.pk/print/495209-pakistan-and-energy-prices
https://www.macrotrends.net/countries/PAK/pakistan/unemployment-rate#
www.macrotrends.net/countries/PAK/pakistan/unemployment-rate

INTOLERANCE, EXTREMISM, AND MORAL DEGRADATION

Intolerance and Extremism

In Pakistan we must promote tolerance in matters pertaining to religion. Our religion clearly says that there would be no compulsion in matters of religion. "Let there be no compulsion in religion ..." (Qur'ān 2:256)

Considering only ourselves right and everybody else wrong promotes intolerance. It is unfortunate that we do not ourselves follow the teachings of Islam especially in terms of rights of other people ("Haqooq ul Ebad") which is compulsory for us.

The white color in our national flag represents minorities and it is our responsibility to provide security to their life and property. Even a cursory glance of Islam shows it to be a religion of mercy to all people, both Muslims and non-Muslims Islam abhors needless killing and exhorts the protection of the lives of entire humanity. The Qur'ān is emphatic: "If you kill an innocent human, it is as though you have killed the entire humanity." (Qur'ān 5:32)

Islam itself teaches moderation, to the extent that Prophet Muhammad ﷺ is depicted as one of the world's "leading law givers" in the US Supreme Court main hall in recognition of the use of the "Charter of Madina" in the US Constitution's Bill of Rights. Few bigoted pseudo religious leaders have distorted the tenets of Islam and preach violence against perceived offenders of the religion.

Extremism is something irrational, unjustifiable and unacceptable to a civil society with common standards of ethics and reciprocity. Extremism could be religious, sectarian, ethnic or fanaticism that is intolerance of people thought to be less religious than some.

It must be remembered that the Holy Prophet Muhammad ﷺ was himself the most tolerant of humans. The case of the infidel old woman, in the days of early Islam could be recounted as an example. She would throw garbage upon the person of the Holy Prophet ﷺ, whenever he would pass her street on his way to prayers, forcing him to go back home and change his clothes. When she did not appear one day to conduct her abhorrent deed, the Holy Prophet ﷺ went to her home to inquire upon her welfare. He discovered that she was lying sick with no one to attend her. The Holy Prophet ﷺ looked after her, and when she regained health, she was so impressed by the Holy Prophet's ﷺ conduct that she converted to Islam. We may also recall the occasion, when during a battle, Hazrat Ali (Razi Allah ho tallah unho) floored an infidel warrior and was about to behead him when he spat on the face of Hazrat Ali (Razi Allah ho tallah unho), who spared his life stating that "I was going to kill you since you were an enemy of Allah, but when you spat on my face, you became my personal enemy and I would not like to take a life on personal enmity".

Controlling Intolerance and Extremism:

For controlling religious tolerance in the country, opinion builders of all shades of life must come forward to play a positive role. Community leaders, intellectuals, politicians, the media, school, college and university teachers all must contribute.

The religious teachers and the Imams of the mosques should be made to realize that they must base their teachings and their speeches or "Khutbas" to desist from hate speech and propagate tolerance in the light of teachings of Islam as practiced by the Holy prophet ﷺ

It needs to be infused in the minds of the common folk that those who attack innocent people or places or shrines of saints are enemies of Islam. The saints like "Hazrat Data Ganj Bakhsh" converted thousands of people to Islam through their love and practice by example.

Long-term reforms could be introduced to include action against publications spreading hate, Madrassa reforms and improvement in religious syllabi besides eliminating extremist organizations

All institutions of state must implement the "National Action Plan" which was jointly agreed by all stake holders including all political parties.

MORAL DEGRADATION
& INDISCIPLINE:

We have reached an abyssal low level of moral degradation and Indiscipline. It has permeated gradually over our history. I would hold the rulers responsible for that as adhering to moral values and following the system and the rules have a trickle-down effect and vice versa.

Today it is quite common among people to earn by unfair means, cheat others, and lie to people to further their interest and not to respect others right or not to fulfill a promise made to others in the society. Total lack of discipline and unwillingness to stand in a que or respect and show courtesy to others has become our hallmark. What a pity that the values prescribed for us by founder of our nation are totally ignored. People generally tend to justify their mad conducts by saying that all others do like that or the high ups in the society do like that.

Today if you go to a vegetable or fruit or meat seller or milk seller, all would try to cheat the others. It is quite common for business like tailoring etc to promise delivery on a particular date but later put it off till several requests or visits by the client. If you go a service provider, especially in public sector he would avoid doing your justified work without gratification.

Look at our parks littered all over with plastic bags food wrappers, disposable water or soda containers and what not. If you look at a cinema hall just after conclusion of a show see the litter rampage. We feel very proud to call over selves Muslims but alas our actions are just the reverse of what we should be doing. Such things were nonexistent or at least much better at a time in history when say we were in high school, in 1950s and early 60s. Also the level of efficiency and quality of public services like transport within city or intercity transport was very good and reliable. In Lahore we used to cherish Lahore Omni Bus Service. It was an efficient, on time, neat service available for travel within city and to outskirts at very affordable cost. Similarly railway was a reliable neat, on time service at affordable cost. So were our air services which provided lead to Middle East.

Organizations like Civil Defense, or SPCA (Society for prevention of cruelty to animals) used to function efficiently and they were very much visible through their work. Such organizations had also visible neat offices and staff.

About adherence to rules I remember that in the 1950s we used to have a dynamo powered light for the cycles. Even" tongas" used to have two side lamps in working order. Any violation would lead to a challan and fine which was very very rare. People used to obey traffic rules and signals strictly. Everything has gone down the drain.

I very well remember I was in class -6 when one day leaving for school in a rush I picked up a pencil from my father's working table. He asked me to put it back as it was for his office work. He said he would not work with it for any personal or domestic work as it comes from his office stationary. He gave me some money and asked me to buy whatever I need from the school stationary shop.

What to do:

The rulers and the elite have to strictly follow the moral values and obey the rules and regulations and avoid using their wealth to make people corrupt or to sabotage the system. System must be developed to come hard on such violations.

People also have to pull themselves up and stop cheating their fellow citizens. Everybody has to rest oneself to respect other people's rights and show courtesy and follow the rules.

The parents must teach ("tarbeeat") their children in moral values like respecting elders, the difference between "hallal" and "haram", between right and wrong, to behave while visiting shops or others homes or not to litter and to follow the rules and respect other peoples' rights etc.

The government must ensure that any violation of rules or any demands for gratification are met with strict punishments.

The government must also endeavor to ask prayer leaders to stress on respecting other people's rights and on how to conduct ourselves in daily life.

References:

http://www.criterion-quarterly.com/no-place-for-extremism-religious-intolerance-in-islam/

https://nation.com.pk/27-Dec-2016/religious-extremism-and-terrorism-in-pakistan

https://www.thenews.com.pk/print/201548-Institutional-decay-moral-decline-hampering-Pakistans-progress

https://www.dawn.com/news/674038ttps://nation.com.pk/27-Dec-2016/religious-extremism-and-terrorism-in-pakistan

EDUCATION

The Need

Constitution of Pakistan envisages free and compulsory education to all children between the ages of 5 to 16 years to enhance literacy. After the 18th constitutional amendment education, was transferred to the provinces. The federating units are now supposed to legislate and design educational policies which ensure quality education.

On the Global Competitiveness Index (GCI) in 2016 the country stands at a low 128 among 138 countries. In higher education and training it is currently ranked 123rd. There are 24 million out-of-school children in Pakistan, the second highest figure in the world after Nigeria

In the recent report by Quacquarelli Symonds (QS), a British higher education ranking agency, that compares the standards of higher education in 50 countries, Pakistan ranks dead last with a score of 9.2. The U.S. and U.K ranked top with scores of 100 and 98.5 respectively, while India stood at 24th with a score of 60.9

Different Types of Education Based on Affordability:

Pakistan has strange discriminatory systems of education. There is a very low quality curriculum designed for the poor including rural population. There is a separate system with curriculum based on English language for the rich who can afford it. Here are the different education system categories:

1. The least privileged children in rural areas study in lack of proper physical infrastructure and shortage rather complete lack of qualified teachers. In recent estimates the shortage of qualified teachers was put at 1.5 million evidently mostly in public sector.

2. The second tier system comprises government schools which teach a low level curriculum. They generally lack quality infrastructure. Also the testing standards in these schools are quite low. These are sometimes kept deliberately low to avoid drop out before ninth class level.

3. In some big cities there exists a system of government run model schools. These schools have good infrastructure, better curriculum and better qualified teachers. It usually provides the main source of education for the children of middle class educated parents. It also includes semi government and NGO assisted schools. Somewhat similar in standards are the schools sponsored by the armed forces.

4. At the top there is a system category for the privileged minority based upon the curriculum taught in British O Level (Ordinary Level) and A Level (Advanced level) system.

There first three categories the education up to class-10 results in grant of Matric certificate for the successful students.

The last category results in grant of O-Level certificate. As compared with Matric, the O-Level education system is superior, more expansive and based on curriculum accepted in the world as a standard. Also English being the medium of education in O-Level, the successful students can have more opportunities for studies worldwide. Similarly the FA or FSC levels coming out of categories 1 to 3 are in competition with A-Level students. In this case also the A-Level successful students have better opportunities worldwide for further specialized education like medical and engineering.

REFORMING EDUCATION

Pakistan urgently needs to evolve and put into practice a unified system of Education where the rich and the poor are coached under a single high quality unified curriculum to be adopted in both private and public sector schools. English as an essential international language has to be adopted as medium of instruction for High School and Higher Secondary level education. The national language must also be made compulsory as a means of preserving our unique culture and heritage.

All private and government run schools must have proper buildings and other infrastructure such as play grounds, halls for such activities as declamation contests, music and drama and other such activities. There should also be two year training of Junior Cadet Corps in Class-9 and 10. This instills discipline and makes young people more tough and alert. Activities like swimming, scouting, inter school competitions have also to be encouraged.

Teachers have to be fully qualified and properly trained. The salaries of teachers have to be enhanced to a level that they are respected in the society and they do not have to look toward earning from tuitions etc.

Parents have to be counselled to guide their children to choose a market friendly career. Drop outs have to be avoided and for that technical education should be made a part of secondary education. Classes for carpentry, electrical works, mechanical works, plumbing etc should be included in the curriculum.

Most higher education buildings in the public sector will have to upgrade their infrastructure. Academic freedom of faculty in the public sector has to be ensured.

A recent UNICEF report estimates that there are around 4 million orphans living in Pakistan. Provincial governments, international organizations and some private organizations endeavor to provide shelter to them. However most of the orphans are residing in Madrasahs. If a universal high quality education standard is to be established, the most vulnerable section of society, the orphans should also be given the same privilege and opportunity. This would lead to a more just and equitable society.

References:

http://www.ipripak.org/education-system-of-pakistan-issues-problems-and-solutions/
https://en.wikipedia.org/wiki/Education_in_Pakistan
http://unesco.org.pk/education/documents/publications/The%20Education%20system%20in%20pakistan.pdf
https://www.researchgate.net/publication/298797040_Causes_Of_The_Decline_Of_Education_In_Pakistan_And_Its_Remedies

https://www.slideshare.net/talhakhan143/educational-standard-in-pakistan

http://moent.gov.pk/mopttm/userfiles1/file/Minimum%20 Standards%20for%20Quality%20Education%20in%20 Pakistan.pdf

http://uis.unesco.org/sites/default/files/documents/secondary-education-regional-information-base-country-profile-for-pakistan-en.pdf

https://www.quora.com/In-Pakistan-Matric-FSc-O-level-and-A-level-are-the-available-education-systems-Which-is-better-for-getting-into-a-professional-university

https://ilm.com.pk/courses/oa-level-courses/difference-between-o-level-and-matric-in-pakistan/

https://www.nuffic.nl/en/publications/find-a-publication/ education-system-pakistan.pdf

http://www.moent.gov.pk/userfiles1/file/National%20 Educaiton%20Policy%202017.pdf

http://www.nust.edu.pk/INSTITUTIONS/Directortes/ GTTN/Download%20Section/GTTN%20Policy%20 Insight%202.pdf

LACK OF DEMOCRATIC PROCESS IN HISTORY

A key to economic success in developed countries has been their practice of democratic systems in earnest. Our country lacked tremendously on this count. We need to understand and analyze the reasons for chaos in countries like Nigeria which had more than ample resources. Also we need to examine what was the difference between Malaysia and Indonesia or say between Iraq and UAE.

In order to understand the problem we have to glance at our history

THE FORMATIVE YEARS (1947-1958), STRUGGLING DEMOCRACY

Pakistan's founding fathers gave a model of Pakistan that was to be welfare state with a modern democratic setup. The common people believed this would be an Islamic welfare state. Unfortunately, as it turned out, it was neither an Islamic welfare state nor a democratic state.

After early death of founder of the nation, the regional political leaders were ignored. They were sons of the soil, having strong social and political bases and were looked upon with respect by sizeable followers. It was perhaps essential to engage the likes of Khan Abdul Ghaffar Khan, Abdul Samad Achakzai, G.M. Syed, and Ghous Baksh Bizenjo for realizing the objects the League had promised.

The civil servants were trained for administering a colonial state. They unfortunately employed the same arrogant and colonial mindset to administer the new independent state.

The fear of Indian threat to the existence of Pakistan led to diverting resources to the military. This fear also led Pakistan into seeking a patron to for its defense and to entrench itself into American cold war camp on the hopes that USA would protect its freedom. Leasing an airbase in Peshawar in 1950s, the Central Intelligence Agency's spy activities grew rapidly. These activities were exposed in 1960 when the Soviet

Union's air defense intercepted and shot down the U-2 plane and captured its pilot. This incident severely compromised the national security of Pakistan that brought the Soviet ire on Pakistan.

The alliance with west led to the military modernizing more rapidly, creating a civil military imbalance. The imbalance resulted in a strong centralized approach denying decentralization of powers to the provinces.

When Ayub Khan became the Commander in Chief of the army, a civil military alliance emerged where lines were drawn very early about who was to be the actual power holder. Liaquat Ali Khan's assassination led to start of political engineering. In complete disregard of parliamentary practices, the cabinet was made to elevate the finance minister, Ghulam Mohammad, to the post of governor general.

In the following years, several rounds of differences and tussles between the governors general and the prime ministers gradually unfurled the relative strength of the former office vis-à-vis the latter.

The federal legislature, which till 1956 also served as the constituent assembly, remained a docile body.

In 1953, the then prime minister Muhammad Ali Bogra (a Bengali) succeeded in finally devising a formula. It suggested representation on the basis of population in the lower house and equal representation for five provinces in the upper house. Seats allocated to each province in the lower house were such that when it joined the upper house with equal seats for all provinces, the joint session of parliament could have equal representation for both the wings of the country.

The prime minister had a series of legislation passed reducing the powers of the governor general. The latter was now prohibited from appointing and dismissing a prime minister at will. Also, to form the government, he was to call upon a person who was a member of the assembly, and who could be removed only by a vote of no-confidence. This annoyed the then Governor General, Ghulam Muhammad and the powers who supported him.

The incoming government had the C-in-C as the defense minister to gather with Iskander Mirza. The new cabinet merged all the provinces and states in the western wing of the country, creating the province of West Pakistan. This was done to neutralize the numerical majority of East Bengal. The country had now only two provinces, East and West Pakistan, having equal representation. The term 'parity' thus entered Pakistan's political lexicon

Ghulam Mohammad's decision of Oct 24, 1954, to dissolve the assembly was declared illegal by the Sindh High Court, which held that the governor general had the right to dissolve the legislative assembly under the interim constitution, but the assembly dissolved by him also served as the constituent assembly, whose dissolution was not within his competence. However, the historic decision was overruled by the federal court which observed that the constituent assembly, by not being able to furnish the constitution in seven years, had lost its legitimacy. Pakistan's judiciary, therefore, derailed the country's constitutional and democratic journey with this decision. Subsequently, the Federal Court and, later the Supreme Court, followed the tradition of un-seating the civilian regimes. But it all started in 1954

In June 1955, a new assembly was elected through the electoral college of the provincial assemblies. By then, the provincial assembly in East Bengal had been re-elected, and in the provincial elections, held in early 1954, the United Front had defeated, rather routed, the Muslim League. The Bengali component of the Muslim League parliamentary party having shrunk, the Bengali prime minister, Mr Bogra, was replaced with Chaudhri Mohammad Ali. The main achievement of Mohammad Ali's government was the approval of the 1956 constitution which brought to an end the dominion status of Pakistan and made it a republic. The background maneuvering continued. The parliamentary system itself was subdued by giving extraordinary powers to the president. This was done only because the last governor general, Iskander Mirza, had to become the first president after the adoption of the constitution.

Mirza lost no time in asking Chaudhry Mohammad Ali to resign. Now Hussain Shaheed Suhrawardy was invited to form the government. The Awami League leader managed to form a coalition, but within 13 months he was shown the door once he failed in keeping the coalition together. Mirza then looked towards Muslim League leader I.I. Chundrigar, who could survive less than two months, losing his office on the electorate issue. Then came Feroz Khan Noon of the Republican Party who managed a coalition with the Awami League that lasted 10 months until Mirza imposed martial law in collaboration with Gen Ayub Khan. Mirza also abrogated the constitution. Within 20 days, Ayub turned the tables on Mirza. Four of Ayub's generals went to President House and forcibly acquired his resignation. Mirza was deported a week later to London where he lived the rest of his life in oblivion. Pakistan, at this point, entered the first phase of its military rule.

MILITARY RULE (1958-1971)

Ayub was candid about his disdain for parliamentary democracy from the very beginning. A highly Western-oriented, Ayub took pride in Pakistan being the United States' 'most-allied ally', and installed a political system that strongly mirrored America's presidential form of democracy.

Ayub's 1962 constitution envisioned an electoral college of 80,000 people who would elect the President. The Basic Democracies system was a multi-layered, complex system that allowed Ayub Khan to be indirectly "elected" as "President". This system also showed Ayub Khan's disdain for Parliamentary democracy. In 1965, Ayub Khan fought elections as PML candidate to counter the popular and famed non-partisan Fatima Jinnah and controversially re-elected for the second term. He was faced with allegations of widespread intentional vote riggings.

In 1959, Ayub Khan made an offer of joint defence with India during the Sino-Indo clashes in October 1959. The move was seen as a result of American pressure and a lack of understanding of Foreign affairs. In 1960, President Ayub signed the Indus Water Treaty with Indian Prime Minister Nehru, giving away full control of three eastern rivers to India. It is well known that Chinese Premier Chou in Li had asked Ayub Khan to take over Indian held Kashmir when India was at war with China in 1962. This was also reported by Ayub Khan's Principal Secretary, Qudrat Ullah Shhab in his book "Shahab Nama".

The war with India in 1965 was a turning point in his presidency, The Operation"Gibralter" was lunched on the presumption that India would not attack Pakistan due to Kashmir being a disputed territory, The presumption obviously proved wrong when India launched a full scale war against West Pakistan attacking Lahore with full force.

Ayub Khan's main sponsor, the United States, did not approve, rather disliked the war move. Kennedy administration placed an economic embargo that caused Pakistan to lose $500 million in aid and grants that had been received through consortium. Ayub Khan could not politically survive in the aftermath of 1965 war.

Public criticism of his personal and sons' wealth increased. One Western commentator in 1969 estimated Gohar Ayub's personal wealth at the time at $4 million, while his family's wealth was put in the range of $10–20 million

Ayub Khan's economic policies gave birth to regional and income inequalities. This inequality, coupled with his stifling of democracy eventually gave birth to the social unrest that forced Ayub to resign in 1969. The former army chief, however, chose not to hold elections and instead passed on the baton to the then army chief, Yahya Khan.

Yahya, though, held direct elections in Pakistan on the basis of 'one person, one vote' but his role in the subsequent political crisis highlights his inherent bias and disdain for sharing power with East Pakistan and for his desire to self-perpetuate himself as the President.

Until 1958 nobody had ever accused the politicians of being corrupt. All of them, right from Liaquat Ali Khan to Feroze Khan Noon, their families and their close relatives lived a normal life while in power or when out of power. None of them has ever been accused of amassing wealth while in power.

DEMOCRACY INTERVENES

(December 1971-July 1977):

The general elections held by Yahya Khan in 1970 resulted in the Awami League winning a majority of seats in East Pakistan and the Pakistan People's Party of Zulfikar Ali Bhutto winning a majority in West Pakistan. The two parties and Yahya Khan were unable to agree on a new constitution and democratic dispensation. Subsequent uprisings led to the secession of Bangladesh, and Pakistan losing the war against Bangladesh-allied India in 1971.

Thus in December 1971 after separation of East Pakistan, the reins of power came to Zulfikar Ali Buhtto in the reaming Pakistan. Bhutto was a highly intelligent person educated at Berkeley and Oxford and trained at as Barrister at the Lincoln's Inn. At this time the Pakistan and its military felt humiliated and devoid of pride. By July 1972, Bhutto had recovered 43,600 prisoners of war and 5,000 square miles of Indian-held territory after signing the Simla Agreement. He strengthened ties with China and Saudi Arabia, recognised Bangladesh, and hosted the second Organisation of the Islamic Conference in Lahore in 1974.

Bhutto's reign saw parliament unanimously approve a new constitution in 1973. A key clause in the 1973 Constitution required members of the armed forces to take an oath promising not to take part in political activities and making it illegal for the military to intervene in politics. Bhutto also played an integral role in initiating the country's nuclear programme.

However, Bhutto's nationalization of much of Pakistan's fledgling industries, healthcare, and educational institutions led to economic stagnation. After dissolving provincial governments in Baluchistan was met with unrest, Bhutto also ordered an army operation in the province in 1973, causing thousands of civilian casualties. Bhutto's democratic and socialist credentials were totally undone. Arrogance and clear signs of intolerance of dissent started emerging in the years 1972-73. He could be a democrat but also mercilessly authoritarian.

The parliamentary elections in 1977 were won by PPP by a wide margin. However, the opposition alleged widespread vote rigging, and violence escalated across the country.

The strong anti-Bhutto movement had acquired an Islamist hue from very early on, and, despite Bhutto making numerous symbolic concessions like banning alcohol, declaring Friday as the weekly holiday, the pressure continued resulting in negotiations between Bhutto and the opposition in early July 1977.

MILITARY RULE AGAIN (1977-1988)

On 5 July 1977, Bhutto was deposed by his appointed army chief General Zia-ul-Haq in a military coup before being controversially tried and executed by the Supreme Court of Pakistan in 1979 for authorizing the murder of a political opponent.

Ziaul Haq. In his speech to the nation on taking over power on July 5, 1977, Gen Zia said he had done so only to defend democracy and for the well-being and survival of Pakistan, that he had no political ambitions whatsoever, and that he would leave his post of Chief Martial Law Administrator (CMLA) after three months – the infamous 90 days – and hand over power to Pakistan's elected representatives.

Zia-ul-Haq abrogated the 1977 Constitution. Supreme Court invoked the Doctrine of Necessity to allow Zia to continue with his actions for years to come.

The Movement for Democracy (MRD) started in August 1983 against Zia ul Haq. The movement activists were brutally attacked by the police all across the country. The protests however resulted in announcement of part-less "elections" in 1985. Through these "elections" Muhammad Khan Junejo was nominated as "Prime Minister". Though he was expected to be subservient, Junejo grew in confidence quite soon. He insisted on lifting the Martial Law and differed with Zia on the end game scenario in Afghanistan. The "National Assembly" was dissolved in May 1988 using 8th amendment which was inserted as a prerequisite for lifting the Martial Law in 1985.

Zia ruled oppressively using a myopic and sycophant view of Islam only to perpetuate his rule. He also took a unilateral and typical dictatorial decision to enter into America's war against Soviet invasion of Afghanistan. This resulted in over 4 million Afghans coming over to Pakistan. UNHCR reported in February 2017 that about 1.3 million registered Afghan citizens still remained in Pakistan. The war effects and authoritarian rule in Pakistan resulted in radicalisation of the society, conservatism, intolerance, extremism, drugs and gun culture. It continues to haunt Pakistan's political and social fabric. His death in August 1988 in plane crash ushered in new curtailed, managed democracy in Pakistan.

CONTROLLED DEMOCRACY WITH OSCILLATING PRIME MINISTERS (1988-1999)

Pakistan's 1990s oscillated between rule by Benazir Bhutto and Nawaz Sharif. Benazir made a remarkable return in 1988 elections when PPP won the elections. However, General Zia's legacy continued to stifle democracy in Pakistan, with Benazir coming in direct conflict with the now far more powerful position of President. It was eighth amendment that paved the way for President Ghulam Ishaq Khan's dismissal of Benazir's government in 1990.

The 1990 elections saw Nawaz Sharif's Islami Jamhoori Ittehad (IJI) coming to power. However his tenure too was marked by conflict with the military and the President. Nawaz made the wise decision to keep Pakistan out of the First Gulf War, and laid the grounds for what would become Nawaz's brainchild—the motorways in his tenure, but his time in office too was cut short when the military forced both him and Ghulam Khan to resign in 1993 after they could not agree on key policy measures.

Next elections in 1993 saw Benazir emerge victorious and in 1996 elections Nawaz Sharif came to power with a a two third majority. That allowed him to pass the Thirteenth amendment that limited the President's powers and finally gave breathing space to civilian rule. In May 1998, Nawaz Sharif allowed conducting of 6 nuclear tests despite strong opposition from country's economic patrons. The resulting sanctions and freezing of foreign currency accounts made him unpopular. He triggered inter-institutional conflict and later when he tried to remove army Chief Pervez Musharraf, the military triggering a military coup. Nawaz Sharif was arrested, convicted for plane hijack and exiled to Saudi Arabia for 8 years.

MILITARY STEPS IN ONCE MORE (1999-2008)

After over throwing an elected government which is a treasonable offence punishable by death according to the Constitution of Pakistan, Musharraf used 9/11 for self-perpetuation just as Zia had used Soviet invasion of Afghanistan for the same purpose. He secured his future by getting into US alliance to fight war on terror unilaterally. Also Pakistani courts were there as always to legitimize him and even to allow him to fiddle with the constitution. He create a King's party of failed and corrupt politicians from Nawaz Sharif's party and PPP to give it a semblance of civil rule and to pursue his "Enlightened Moderation". After pressure from the religious right he allowed the Seminary education "Dars e Nizami" as equivalent to bachelors' degree so as to enable them to contest his graduate only "elections". This brought a subservient "parliament" and the Muthidda Majlis e Amal (MMA) into power in Khyber Pakhtunkhwa. Musharraf used the MMA's presence in KPK as a bargaining chip with the USA.

In the year 2007, Musharraf oozing with confidence, confronted the once supportive superior judiciary. He soon found himself in a tight corner as the lawyers all over the country agitated strongly.

On 12th May 2007 evening he showed his true dictatorial colors by supporting the day long carnage of killing several dozen innocent people in Karachi who wanted to receive the Chief Justice at Karachi airport. This gave impetus to the lawyer's movement against him. The Lal Masjid event and the participation in "war on terror" resulted in worst wave of domestic terror which left an estimated 70,000 people dead.

In October, Musharraf signed the National Reconciliation Ordinance (NRO), granting amnesty to many prominent politicians, a further sign of his weakening grip on power. On November 3, Musharraf imposed a desperate mini-martial law and declared emergency. The killing of Akbar Bugti created Baluchistan crisis which further weakened his hold on power. Benazir Bhutto and Nawaz Sharif had returned to the country and were challenging Musharraf under the banner of a Charter of Democracy. Pervez Musharraf was forced out by democratic forces in 2008.

DEMOCRACY GAINS HOLD (2008-PRESENT)

After assassination of Benazir Bhutto in December 2007, her widower Asif Ali Zardari became a heir apparent. The elections in February 2008 saw PPP and PML (N) getting most of the National Assembly seats. Both parties formed a coalition government but soon PML (N) parted ways and PPP ruled the rest of the 5 year tenure. After forcing out Musharraf, Zardari was elected President of Pakistan. Zardari mostly worked coolly perusing a policy of reconciliation.

During most of the PPP term, judicial activism was at its peak. Two Prime Ministers were disqualified by the Supreme Court. However both PPP and PML (N) worked for collective democratic good to pass 18th Amendment to the Constitution, renaming the NWFP as Khyber Pakhtunkhaw and deciding on the National Finance Commission (NFC) award. It was through a democratic moment of reconciliation and equity by which PML (N) government in the Punjab reduced its share in the NFC, giving a greater share to the less-privileged provinces.

At the end of 5 years the PPP passed on power from one democratic government to another, PML (N) which won majority of seats in the 2013 elections.

One of the parting acts of the PPP government was the initiation of legal proceedings against Pervez Musharraf for high treason. The former army chief subsequently had to appear in court for a few times before he was allowed to proceed abroad apparently for medical treatment.

After taking over power in end of May 2013, Nawaz Sharif had to confront the allegations of rigging by PTI through a 120 days sit-in in Islamabad. The PPP supported the democratically elected government despite having reservations on transparency of polls. Events like reopening of Musharraf's trial, "Dawn Leaks" etc resulted in tension with the Military. After Panama Papers mentioned about Nawaz Sharif and his children having high value properties in England, judicial activism was apparent on perusing the case against him and on governance issues. He was eventually disqualified for life by the Supreme Court for non-disclosure of an income.

A separate case in Accountability Court convicted Nawaz Sharif for ten years imprisonment and his daughter for 7 years rigorous imprisonment before scheduled election of July 2018.

PML (N) government however completed its 5 year term until end of May 2018. Elections on 25th July 2018 gave Imran Khan's PTI the largest number of seats followed by PML (N) and PPP. Presently the transition to third consecutive democratically elected government has been completed.

QUALITY OF POLITICIANS

To understand about quality of available politicians in Pakistan we again have to have a glance at our history. **Few facts are evident from Pakistan's history:**

Pakistan's first Prime Minister, Liaquat Ali Khan remained the Prime Minister for 4 years, 2 months, 2 days. After the assassination of, Liaquat Ali Khan in 1951, there were seven different Prime Ministers within a period of six years.

Zulfikar Ali Bhutto was the PM for 3 years 10 months 21 days. Yousaf Raza Gillani served the maximum, the longest period for 4 years, 2 months 2 days. Benazir Bhutto's two terms aggregate to 4 years 8 months, 21 days. Nawaz Sharif's 3 terms aggregate into a total period of 5 years, 2 months, 27 days.

The politicians (Prime Ministers and Governor Generals) up to 1958 were not corrupt. They did not increase their net worth or their families' net worth While in power. Zulfikar Ali Bhutto has also never been accused of any financial wrong doing or increasing his assets while in power.

The self-imposed rulers, their families, their relatives, and their mentored politicians are very well known to increase their assets and their net worth while in office. Ironically Yahya Khan was an exception.

It is well known that post 1977, projects impacting general public like availability of electricity and gas, like infrastructure development were undertaken only during democratically elected leaders. During long periods under self-imposed rulers from 1977-1988 and from 1999-2008, the focus was only on pleasing the USA for self-perpetuation. None of them ever thought of getting Pakistan's debt to USA waved off as Anwar Sadat did for Egypt. None of them thought of putting up a high impact decision on the "Parliament".

The 22nd Prime Minister of Pakistan, Imran Khan was sworn-in in July 2018. He has been known to be an honest person and people trusted his philanthropic undertakings. Now as in March 2022 after four years of his rule, people generally feel disappointed. The main reasons of disappointment are: high inflation, un-imaginable increase in electricity and gas bills increasing economic woes, lopsided, inconclusive accountability and lack of reforms which people had expected would change the system. People expected end of status quo which has not come about. There have been questions on his team regarding conflict of interest and mafias running unchecked. This is very unfortunate and political analysts have to think deeply on the causes of the disappointments and think about remedies needed for course correction. Unfortunately some national institutions who try to manage the things in good faith get the blame. It would be advisable for them to keep away from running and managing the system.

The superior courts have a great responsibility in insuring continued running of the democratic system and "accountability" in a fair and impartial manner.

Another unfortunate aspect has been the recent extreme division bordering on hate among the people based on political following and the views they hold. All stake holders must endeavor to lower the temperature and level of hate. All institutions must also try to heal the extreme divide and unify the people. Failure to do so could have dangerous consequences.

WHAT IS THE REMEDY?

Have Patience, Let Democracy do the Sieving:

Using an analogy, if we make up a cricket team from Germany the players have to be clumsy since the game has not been played there. Similarly the politicians mentored by self-imposed rulers had to be clumsy and they were. Democracy is a sieving process which would bring in better persons with more elections. We have already demonstrated that by progressively electing relatively better leaders. The results of recent July 2018 elections is a vivid example of the tenacity and sharp and deep understanding of the people's will to elect a better, honest person who they think can deliver.

Policy Making be Left to Elected Leaders:

Now that democracy is taking hold with 3rd elected government in place until year 2023, the level of governance and policy making should improve. It has to be remembered that an elected leader has have to deliver as he or she has to face the electorate. All internal and external policies have to be left to the Prime Minister and his team. They must debate and formulate the policies in the Parliament. Security related issues and other selected issues can be discussed first in constitutionally created platform before debate and finalization in the Parliament. This should include handling of affairs about Baluchistan and FATA.

Transparency in Elections is a Must:

Holding of elections in a fare, free and transparent manner, is the only responsibility of Election Commission of Pakistan. It has to have strong, impeccable people. They must ensure a level playing field for all political parties prior to and during elections. The record until now has been somewhat controversial. The courts, and institutions like NAB should ensure that the judgements and actions cannot be perceived, rightly or wrongly to favour some and discriminating for others.

The recent, July 2018 election and the elections previous to them have been somewhat controversial. This must be avoided henceforth by making them absolutely transparent. We must understand the perception that the elections are engineered and managed by some state institutions must come to an end. This causes most undesirable friction and blame game by the masses. This is very much against national interest and must end henceforth.

The counting of votes at all polling stations has to be completed within 1-2 hours. The result at each polling station must be complied on prescribed forms with the signature of all polling agents. This then must be transmitted electronically immediately to the constituency Returning officer, to the Election Commission and to the media. The consolidation of all results in the constituencies must be done within 3 hours in a transparent way which is visible to all parties and to the media.

References:

https://dailytimes.com.pk/247440/a-brief-history-of-pakistans-turbulent-democratic-and-political-evolution/
https://en.wikipedia.org/wiki/Democracy_in_Pakistan
https://www.britannica.com/biography/Mohammad-Ayub-Khan#ref129208
http://www.criterion-quarterly.com/the-tale-of-democracy-in-pakistan/
http://gcaol.com/pakistan-affairs-complete-history-1947-2017-dawn-special-reports/
https://en.wikipedia.org/wiki/Zulfikar_Ali_Bhutto
http://insider.pk/national/list-of-prime-ministers-of-pakistan-since-1947-with-photos/

LACK OF CLEAN DRINKING WATER AND NON FOCUS ON AGRICULTURE

Lack of Clean Drinking Water

All over Pakistan the population does not have access to clean drinking water. This is again a sad example of breakdown of our system that once existed. Rich who can afford to spend consume mineral water in cities and towns. Some boil the water for drinking. In rural areas the situation is much worse. No government has thought about this basic necessity for people.

I remember when I and my wife visited Vienna in summer of 1996; we frantically searched to buy non aerated mineral water in super markets in the city. We could not find it. When I asked an Austrian friend he told me that tap water is drinkable in Vienna. No wonder Vienna is still rated as number one city in the world for living.

WHAT TO DO

The government must work to provide clean drinking water to all urban and rural population. Water filtration units using reverse Osmosis system or any other reliable system should be installed at each union council level. Also they have to be regularly maintained regarding change of filters and membranes to keep the water usable and drinkable. Provision of this basic necessity would also save people especially children from common diseases like diarrhea, ulcers, hepatitis, etc.

Help could be taken from international organizations such as UNDP, WHO etc to fund this project on aid not on loan. Very rich people in Pakistan can also come to finance this basic necessity. A consortium of overseas Pakistanis could also be setup up to finance and maintain the system.

Agricultural Reforms:

Pakistan is basically an agricultural country. Economy of the country very much depends upon agriculture. There has been a total lack of focus on development of agricultural since several decades. We very much need to care about this sector. Following measures are suggested in this regard to perk up agriculture. A task force can be put in place to know the real problems and their solutions through involving farmers.

- Income from agriculture should remain tax free.
- Prices of produce from the main Crops like wheat and cotton are fixed to enable the farmers to earn reasonable profits.
- Adoption of solar and other energy saving methods for tube wells or provision of electricity at lower rates.
- Integrated land management and continuous water management.
- Agricultural research must reach the farmer through provision of improved seeds and plant protection methods.
- Crop Insurance for climatic risks should be available at affordable rates.
- Eliminating middle man and facilitating the transfer of produce to the cities for direct selling.
- Use of Mechanized farming and easy installments or loans to buy such tools
- Introducing dairy farming, Fish Farming, Bee Keeping, cattle and horse farming
- Setting up value added industries near rural areas.

All these measures would help curb movement of rural people to cities for earning livelihood.